LANTERN

First published in 2019
by Offord Road Books

www.offordroadbooks.co.uk

Typeset by Offord Road Books
Printed in the UK by Palace Printers

ISBN 978–1–999–93049–3

1 3 5 7 9 10 8 6 4 2

Lantern

SEÁN HEWITT

Leaf

for woods are forms of grief
grown from the earth. for they creak

with the weight of it.
for each tree is an altar to time.

for the oak, whose every knot
guards a hushed cymbal of water.

for how the silver water holds
the heavens in its eye.

for the axletree of heaven
and the sleeping coil of wind

and the moon keeping watch.
for how each leaf traps light as it falls.

for even in the nighttime of life
it is worth living, just hold it.

Barn Owls in Suffolk

I watch them for a long while,
the pair rising and courting the field
in daylight, the strange geometry
of their faces funnelling the air,

and everything – their whiteness,
their sense of having slipped
through from another world,
their focus on the hunt –

in the end it all comes down
to their silence –
the way each feather disperses
the air, how each wavers –

and I wonder what omen it is
to see two barn owls hunting
in mid-morning, so quietly
secretive, for surely

there is something in the slow
spread of the wing, the moment
of inverted flight, the living thing
pulled from the earth and lifted.

Ilex

Distracting myself, waiting for news,
I walked until I saw this white cluster
of holly growing at the base of a tree,

the stems yellowed, the angled clutch
of leaves like a bleached coral, a pale
antler, almost medieval, like a relic

unearthing in the gloom of the wood.
Later, still the baby would not latch,
and I came back to this holly, unhardened

by the sun, unable to turn the light
into strength. May it keep its whiteness,
may it never learn the use of spikes;

or, in time, when a crown is made of it,
may the people approach one by one
to witness how a fragile thing is raised.

Oak Glossary

in the language of the oak, *sky*
is made by shivering the leaves
to produce a hushing sound.
in winter, of course, *sky* is silent.

god is felt in the phloem and xylem
as a deep echo of water – a low noise
that must be observed by placing
an ear to the bark. for oaks, *chanting*

(which is akin to *song*) is produced
via rhythms of air brought in and out
of the branches in slow succession.
on still days, *song* is not possible.

the familiar words, such as *child*,
man, *woman*, are unknown, having
fallen quiet from disuse. in oak,
essential nouns include *soil*,

water and *time* – these are produced
from their elements. *water* is a high
and gentle noise of clearest quality
which results from branches dripping.

for *soil*, or *earth*, a fastening of the roots
can be felt as a low tension underfoot.
time, on the other hand, is more visual
than aural, and is distinguished into

its linear and circular conceptions.
as is well-known, *circular time*
in oak is communicated
most vividly at the site of a knot

or where the core has been exposed.
the linear variety is felt only
on occasion. for this, sap is produced
and is made to run from the body.

Kyrie

Purple blush of sky and lilac drooping
by the greenhouse. The last heat of day
rests in the grass, and from the shadows
under the conifers, there comes a moaning,

a pain riddling from the undergrowth,
a voice caught out after dark. And my mind,
closed off from sight and the body's reading
of the world, convinces me it is the crying

of a child left out in the yard behind ours.
Naked, its soft fat limbs and wet mouth open
and wailing and helpless. I stand frozen
by the back door and the quiet house,

trying to listen, receptive but distrusting
my body – the ring of light from the kitchen
over my shoulder making of the garden
a more solid darkness beyond the patio,

like the darkness that lives behind eyelids.
I swear at first the crying seems to stop
my heart as I think of it, sends my mind
whirring outwards into the night. Trance-like,

I begin to move further from the light
of the window, slow enough
for my eyes to reinterpret with each step
the shapes of bushes, the forms of shirts

hanging on the line, but still I cannot imagine
the sound as anything but a child cursing
in the pitch-dark conifers. As I walk closer,
my hands white in the garden air, a sudden

panic breaks in the bushes, a brawling,
and I see the darker shapes of two cats
mating. It is here, by the swaying trees,
away from the glow of the house,

that I realise I have found myself at a place
so close to life, to its truth of violence,
that my mind has wired out, but even now
I could not say which was the truer thought:

the cats or the lost child; and I think again
of calling home that night from Sweden,
of hearing my mother's voice and telling her
what you had done (tablets, rum, calling

to say goodbye), and how I made
an animal sound, a noise so primitive
that I felt inhuman, how I cried
like something new-born

because I had found myself
in a world where all abstract things
(death, fear, loss) had bloomed in my mind,
and what is a parent to a child but a god

who we turn to when we still believe
that everything is fixable, a god
who we weep to as we grow
into the world, as we age into it

and each abstraction comes closer.
And now I am back in the garden,
staring into the conifers, the kitchen light
receding from my shoulders,

and considering all the ways
a mind can uproot itself,
all the short-circuits left in the world.
I am thinking of the shadows

under trees, the lives of animals,
the places where words extinguish
themselves and leave all the things
that cannot be fixed or forgotten.

Moor

is childless, sulks
speaks rain and sudden light

is a mind
is sleepless, lies deep in its bed
is always moving about at night

speaks fog with its moss-mouth
is turned to sea by the wind
is waves in the dark, crashing

is suddenly still
is a trembling of light on the tent
is a shudder of guy-ropes and a shadow passing
is kept awake by its conscience

is always waiting,
sounds like breathing, sounds like
it is carrying bodies at night
when no one is watching

is a swallower of sound
wants every night to reach up
and swallow the moon, swallow something

is a mouth
hides and is never caught
sits in the dark quietly and smiles

as the farmer walks out
again with his torch-beam
calling and calling a name

Dormancy

Delicate, grown old in its separation,
a wych elm can send itself to seed,
can sow from its body these translucent

frailties. Just so, visiting you on the ward
where death had been taken, locked
into the matron's safe. You who knew

how separate a person is, how deep
a root can search into darkness
unobstructed. After seeing you

so sexless, unable, I sowed myself
like a wych elm in a windless room.

Härskogen

Each night I would drive this way:
the beam of the headlights tracking
over the effigies of pines, the radio
threatening to falter with each
deepening turn. The lane was long,
lined with rows of towering fir, higher
than any hope of star or half-spent
moon. A lost city, a mind unmoving
in its meditation, the deer left to walk
their shadows among the trees.

Each night, leaving you
in the hospital, I dared myself
to pull over, to switch the engine off.
The cold air would hold me, beating,
in its tourniquet, and the mist would sink
and lift untethered through the beams.
Then, one by one, each tree
would take focus: the cracked age
of the lower bark, violence of the snapped
branch-crown. Everything was silenced

by the endless stretching upwards, life
lifted a little further over my head.
Then behind this tree, many hundreds more
of equal size and strength, and the lakes
freezing gradually in the dells. But here,
only this pine, this circle of trees, one of many
quiet circles. And I would stand thinking
of you, smelling the sap well up from the wounds
and watching the mist, like an old dog,
trying over and over to settle at my feet.

December

I imagine winter returning as if woken from a dream,
clambering from the iced rabbit-hole of the field,
open-mouthed. The sound it makes coming home
knee-deep in the night. Its slow feet, the numb toes.

I listen for the pain in the white shins of the birches,
splinter-trees charred by cold, limbs creaking.
What is the sound of winter? Bark dropping wetly
beneath the laid-down lace of the snow.

And where does it go? To the scales of the fish
which are its sequins, to the frost-skin of the pond
where it grows itself, to the branches of the water
in which it sits, spinning its own white body.

And I will lay down a votive
to my silver birch

for through him all things are made
for his arms are open and are selfless
for he anoints the sick
for witches' brooms are caught in his branches
for he is the light in a darkened wood
for in his way he is the maker of heaven and earth
for he frames the sky and connects it to the earth
for he marks with prayers each hour of the day
for he concludes each day with a choral evensong
for he is a home to many and is welcoming
for his flowers are wingèd
for through him I am granted intercession
for he speaks on my behalf
for his knots are holy fonts
for I can bless myself by him
for he does not observe liturgical time
for his roots allow the resurrection of the dead
for he is scarred with diamonds
for he is the first to return after fire or drought
for he is the improver of soil quality
for he is the friend of wood sorrel and primrose
for he is the friend of moth and woodcock and nightingale
for his body is an instrument of the wind
for he is pure and purifying
for he is vulnerable to fungal pathogens
for he grows quickly but without ambition

for he loses his leaves with the year
for he can pass as a woman
for often his skin takes the pink of dawn
for he has a weeping sister
for he is white but not rare
for he moves
for he does not move

Petition

Clattering down to the bank of the pond
from the wet rocks – soil of the little island
turning underfoot, the tree-roots slick

with rain – and the light is only enough
to make out a few bats, a willow
leaning down to touch the water,

just enough to see how each thing
is altered. On my knees, I put my hand
into the dark of the pond, watch it open

like a white flower. Are we all
just wanting to see ourselves
changed, made unearthly? Tonight,

it seems like everything is trying
to get close to the water –
the willow, the hanging ash –

and as usual, on the opposite bank,
the night-fishermen are sitting
with their torches, lines held out,

waiting for a sign. Just now,
it starts to rain: I watch the pond
pock and sting – its sheet a patience

held for too long – and I, down
on my knees with the pond,
at eye-level with it, watch it breaking;

and the world is down on its knees
beside me – the sky, the rain shattering
its own image and mine. Once,

I queued for the baths
at the sanctuary at Lourdes, was sent
to a room full of frail men undressing:

just a damp white curtain between us
and the icy water rising up
from the Gave de Pau, the deep chant

of a Latin rosary, how a French voice
called to me. Two men inside, a crucifix
on the wall above the stone bath, my towel

taken off. I was given, instead, a sheet
of cotton to wrap around myself,
as though to reassure me that I could be loved

when all my parts were bound together.
All I can remember now is being held
(one hand on my chest, another pressed

to my back); the slow meeting of water
over my body, how the rhythm
of the voices and the river seemed

to reassemble my life around me.
And now the rain is smashing down
into the pond – this is it, I think:

I came here to see myself shattered
and remade, if only to show myself
that it is possible, and the moon

has turned my skin to silver,
and the willow with its head laid down
on the water is whispering something

in its sleep. I get up, pull myself
through the trees: snowberry,
hazels, thistles, bracken . . .

It is so black I can barely see myself
anymore – as I walk it is as though
I am leaving my body by the pond's

moonlit edge – and I wonder what creatures
will come to the water when I have left
(to drink, to feel themselves made whole

by drinking), will find me, will live
beyond my knowledge of them.
For now, the park is so black I am almost

swimming in it, and I only notice
how, from underneath, the trees are all
interlocking (the night-fishermen

casting out again, muttering) –
the night's focus, how everything
is reaching down into the earth

or into the water, each thing quietly
at its work, trying to bring some life
up to the surface, unharmed.

Waterlily

glory be to the *näckros*, naked rose,
open rose, white flower of water.

glory be to water, held in dropped-
stone-ripple, thickened to the green

pad of a leaf. & in time
let us praise the spread

of all anchored things.
praise to the long pale roots

& the chain of water. & let us
take this flower, its quiet face

on the surface & its searching
root as the mystery of faith.

glory be to the work of the pond
& to silt, to the white

open flower which is an offering
& will be given up for us.

Häcksjön

running barefoot, green moss lit
between trees, I go one foot after
the other, arriving on instinct
between roots, dodging

with white feet the white slugs
swelled on forestlight, and you
disappear ahead of slanting pines –
my pale step padding on this sloping

peat path that sinks like a trapdoor
underfoot, and then I leap . . . I love
to plunge through the black glass
of the lake, to make it echo

with my body, feeling the water's
cold resistance . . . for a long moment
I plumb its dark core, and then its arms
rush in and lift me back to the light.

Evening poem

First the clatter-iron blackbird,
its fanatical shuddering in the magnolia.

Dusk; and the garden is reassembling,
calling its sparrows home,

and what a voice-racket under the aucuba
(doors closing to) and each sparrow

an iron-filing sweeping the field-lines
of the garden. I sit out in the last warmth

and watch it all come to rest:
the light falling, the thrushes settling

in the sycamores at the far end
of the lawn, how each tree lowers itself

under a new weight, and I hold out
for a while for everything to darken,

for the birds to stop singing, as though
I am teaching myself again to bear it.

Clock

A close warm evening opened by rain –
and me (caught out) leaning on a cedar.

A heron walks its white zed
along the bank and out into the water,

and just here a small beetle, sheening
coal-black, pulls itself into the pink bed

of the rhododendron flower. Then, once
and once more, a fox barks –

and, though I love you and I know
there is no such thing as held time,

this tree seems suddenly like a stillness,
a circle of quiet air, a place to stand

now that I have had to leave
and cannot think where I might go next.

Wild Garlic

Out in the copse after rain
(too late after dark to be here).
Warm soil, woodlice dripping
from the underside of leaves.

I root down to the tender stalks
and twist them free – soaked petals
dip and touch my arm, kernels
of bud, itch of foliage, of wildness

on my skin. The plants are carrying
the smell, earth-rich, too heavy
to lift above head-height, and my boots
and jeans are bleached with it.

I turn home, and all across the floor
the spiked white flowers
light the way. The world is dark
but the wood is full of stars.

Acknowledgements

Thanks are due to the editors of the following magazines and anthologies in which some of these poems first appeared: *And Other Poems*, *IV Anthology*, *The London Magazine*, *The Manchester Review*, *Magma*, *New Statesman*, *The Poetry Review*, *Resurgence & Ecologist*, and the *Rialto*.

A selection of these poems won a Northern Writers' Award in 2016. Thanks are also due to Arts Council England, for a Grant for the Arts in 2014, and to The Poetry Trust for an Aldeburgh Eight bursary in 2015. 'Ilex' was the winner of the Resurgence Prize in 2017.

Thanks to Andrew McMillan, for his constant generosity, insight and patience, and to others who gave their time to my early drafts: Helen Tookey, Okey Nzelu, Sarah Hymas. Thanks to my parents, for their unending support, and to Will, for letting me write some of these poems. Thanks, too, to Martha Sprackland, for her diligence, precision and attentiveness in editing this manuscript.